Also by **Pamela** *Alexander*

Navigable Waterways

Pamela Alexander

Commonwealth of Wings

An Ornithological

Biography

Based on the Life of

John James Audubon

Wesleyan University Press

Published by University Press of New England

Hanover and London

WESLEYAN UNIVERSITY PRESS
Published by University Press of New England, Hanover, New Hampshire 03755

I would like to thank the Bunting Institute of Radcliffe College for a fellowship, during which I began this project. I am also grateful to those who provided helpful comments on the manuscript, along with encouragement: Wendy Battin, John G. Case, Martha Collins, Laura Fargas, Jorie Graham, Linda Gregerson, Jay Klokker and Gary J. Quigley. This book is for my mother and father.

"Sight" appeared in *Field* as "Audubon Remembers American Falls"; "At Coueron. My First Gun," "Inventory. Journal," and "Aboard the *Ripley*" in *Margin* as "Audubon at 13, as Revolution Begins in France," "Audubon Takes Inventory," and "Audubon aboard the *Ripley*"; "Letter to Victor," "Losses" (2), and "Reprise" (1) in *Michigan Quarterly Review*; "Arrangements," "My Ornithology Proceeds," "I Imagine Thee," and "Return" appeared in *Shankpainter 30*.

Imagine a landscape wholly American, trees, flowers, grass, even the tints of the sky and the waters, quickened with a life that is real, peculiar, trans-Atlantic. It is a real and palpable vision of the New World, with its atmosphere, its imposing vegetation, and its tribes that know not the yoke of man. On twigs, branches, bits of shore, copied by the brush with the strictest fidelity, sport the feathered races, in the size of life, each in its particular attitude, its individuality and peculiarities. The sun shines athwart the clearing in the woods; the swan floats suspended between a cloudless sky and a glittering wave; strange and majestic figures keep pace with the sun.

—Philarete-Chasles, of Audubon's work, 1826

Contents

I. 1785-1803

II. 1803-1808

III. 1808-1826

Commonwealth of Wings

Audubon Enfant

I First
met the light and shook it
Aux Cayes, my mother la créole Rabin
who dies. I am one. Father finds
for me a stepmother and they
together a half-
sister, Muguet called Rosa,
& he is away. In his fields
I cut pieces of cane for me & Rosa
to suck. I am Jean.
My father *marin* learned
this language in an English prison.
Later I count my days from France sometimes,
this place Saint Domingue *maman* hard
to remember. New

world it is, my warm
island, wilderness churning
beyond the lines of coffee plants. The woman
names me again *Fougère* you would say Fern,
names are charms and we need them.
There are places I cannot take the little one.
Edges of things are dangerous—where
sea and land meet, or field and forest,
things get loose from their names.
On the edge of my family I call myself
LaForêt my first self before I knew
French or african or english words.
I saw red birds sign themselves in air
before they sang, flourishing.
"Parroquet. Trogon." She carried me outdoors
& I reached for them, my stepmother said.
I am Jean Jacques Fougère LaForêt Rabin
Audubon.

We Lose St. Domingue

My island has been gone for days, it shrank & flattened
& then sank like a skimmed stone. Rosa
chuckled along with the water & didn't notice.
Father calls them rooster tails, the white arcs
our ship trails at her fastest, when he is happy
& says the waves are French
because they wear berets. We lean
into the wind, we lean to France because
the island darkened, the servants
muttered among themselves & wouldn't answer.
Now I have no place to go. The waves march past us
in rows, & talk, & make a chorus
behind my father's stories, who never said so much
ashore. Birds balance on the wind beside our sails
or make chevrons on the big shoulders of clouds
so they are captains. He says
France will show me new animals & birds
and I will have as many islands as I want,
I'll jingle them like pocket change, he says I am
his little archipelago,
& I think how far we are going,
how big the world will be when we stop.

Nantes, the Revolution

Nantes. Geography, music
threaten daily, *école*.
Four different seasons,
& rabbits & Larks are shy,
no sugar birds here to pick
insects from furniture, neatly.
Buildings dress in uniform,
steep slate roofs the same blues
& grays as pigeons that settle
& scatter hourly from spires
where metal flowers swing
& bang. Windows close to keep outside

out, where I find
muskrats, watch their whiskers move
& the color of their fur
change as it dries. Meetings,
loud talk, then not school but
siège, the city slams shut, bells are unmounted
& melted for cannon, the mouths of waterspouts
taken from squares, coffins raised & opened
for their lead. That is bad, will bring
the dead among us & no one here knows the words
to sing or where to pick the cleansing herbs.
Guns mark the hours now, raggedly,
some so close that when they speak my body rings
& I am disconnected, float
without hearing my boots hit
the stone street where I am fastest among grandfathers
& bell-shaped women. My paper boat rides
to the current, I race along the bank

& find him & fight still
as I do for animals but

there is nothing to scare, only
man-shape in wet clothes, in reeds, it doesn't matter
his mouth is full of mud.
Old men bury him & he is not
the last I find
this spring.

The Siege Outlasted,

life is worse. Shivering royalists stand
at the cathedral wall, those who faint
are shot first
so not to be overlooked.
Townspeople watch but only the muskets clap.
Flies come long before the carts. Loads
are thrown into the Loire until the current slows
then dropped midstream
but the bodies make another bridge below,
& swell, & won't budge. We have
no other place. Fevers take
as many, more, than bullets, & death seems less
because there are many.

At Coueron. My First Gun.

Mama & I
& Rosa, we hope never to meet
another war. Here
the land is flat & trim, sheep
swerve together, hedges & fences
keep order. I explore
margins & flawed places
while Rosa's piano turns
a pretty flurry. I take chocolate
in waxy papers & a basket
to bring back nests & lichens, more strange
than my lessons. The daily murders of the city are far, fewer,
then stop, & I forget them.

We grow
apart, my sister
and I, she domestic, says
my blown eggs & stuffed birds
stink. I close the door.

I shoot well, corks I toss
come down in showers, my fingers gleam
with powder. The gun kicks my shoulder,
its shout & smell clear me.
The bird falls,
always. I watch its color & shine & flare
for weeks before I fire, but my sketch preserves
only its deadness. I burn
my pencil's generation of cripples
on my birthday.

Sometimes I sleep
near my Originals, on leaf litter

beneath the trees they close their eyes in,
sometimes I lie awake in the quiet house
& listen to the nightwatch
kept by the river, old water clock,
& by whickering horses standing
to their sleep.

Father's Home,

leg-wounded, lung-sore, *lieutenant de vasseau*
pensioned. Puts the box of medals in the bottom of his trunk,
sits in the courtyard by the orangery
and dozes when the sun is on him. White petals
fall & mingle with his hair.
The chair tilts on the flags, he starts awake
and finishes reading. Each letter
makes the news bad & worse, finally
the plantation in St. Domingue is lost
complete. La Gerbetière, this place
of limestone walks & box-maze, parterre & pigeon lofts,
has two journals of land. With a farm called Mill Grove
in Pennsylvania, America, it is his last fortune.

His mind is busy with wars. The world
is always burning somewhere, he says:
he smells it. He has a sip of wine
& coughs again, and says he fears
my conscription. I will hide, pockets full
of shot & powder, chalk, paper, cheese—
he shakes his head too slowly to mean No.

We Are Gentlemen Abroad

My French partner's passport's
Dutch, I'm native to New Orleans
to escape Napoleon's levies,
to which

our ship struck by privateers & stripped
of wine, pigs, our best two sailors,
& kept in *Rattlesnake*'s lee
a day, in pistol range,
off Sandy Hook New York

is trifling.

Landed,
sunburned & excited,
I learn that the body remembers
motion: rooms & streets swoop
seawise. I laugh at my sailor's walk
but am suddenly weak—

burning, I ride
long arcs, moan, crest
in sunlight & slide, dizzy, down. Is it water
makes such huge noise? Some
dark thing looms, I struggle,
drenched, in a disarray of quilts—

So my English comes pirated,
fevered, Quakered. They wear
gray dresses, & when they open windows
trees waver in ordinary light
& I am John James, agent

in America for Audubon *père*
who is words on paper here,
an Atlantic of days away
from Rozier & me, men of business.

II. 1803–1808

Mill Grove

My life is curious, immense, unruled
as its new country in which my father's wars
mutter only in the occasional basso
among the river's many voices. High in one rocky bank
I find a large dry cave and draw there;
a phoebe finds it too, then another.
Their conversations transpire
above the pink bells of anemones, above trilliums
white & red. I follow the creek
called Perkiomen. I follow deer trails
& bear tracks & birdsong,
I follow currents of air. Soon every tree
knows my name, the cane brake rattles
to attention! I draw from life now
& finish nothing, dissatisfied, make outlines
of hundreds of flying swifts and finches,
lively but incomplete, & fill my book
with the cooperative faces of my neighbors
the Bakewells. He, William, though english,
is a good shot and possessed
of handsome daughters, excellent
pointer dogs, and a son Thomas. Around us the woods cool
& flare with foxes, the Schuylkill River
hardens for our skating parties
& we are rampant.

The Englishman's Eldest Daughter

We watched, Lucy Bakewell and I,
through the open window
in the drawing room at Fatland Ford,
her father's pillared home I call the Parthenon
to her. Within inches of the sill
the nesting Wren takes ants and spiders,
still struggling, from her mate's bill.
When he flies into the room
& sings, I slide the sash down gently
and he lets Lucy
touch him; Lucy holds him in her hand.

Balancing

I have always slept the way I ride, dance, and shoot—
when I want, and well. Tonight
sleep is harder than waking,
my muscles at ready as if for danger, here
at midnight on the edge of an obscure continent
with my house and farm holding me,
quiet. My heart startles me, its surging so close
to the surface. Is it always so? To put
the parts of sleep together I tell
my muscles one by one to be loose. Why should I not
sleep? I was sick once, my fever on landing,
but I have never been afraid.
My heart slows. Under my hand it kicks

evenly, like a boy sitting on a wooden bridge
who swings his lower legs as if walking
on the green current below
while he thinks he is not afraid, thinks
he doesn't mind that his friends have slid out of sight
leaving him perched, alone, *too high!* although
he saw the water accept and then
hold the others up, saw their backs gleam
in the dark river, their heels
graze the surface from beneath in a slow flutter,
although he knows from lesser jumps
that the rush of water past his ears will sound
like applause—

falling, I wake.

The Current

Lucy, look at that root
diverting the current, leaving a still place
where water & bank fit together
perfectly, the water rising slightly
around each stone to hold it, intimate
as a nest around a dove. See
the green rays that the sun behind us draws
on the water, rays streaming outward
from the shadows of our heads
as if we were painted saints, see
when we move closer we perceive
each other's radiance more clearly? Closer.

Letter to Lucy

Pennsylvanian earth resembles us—
red flesh veiny with water, perfused
with motion & stirred by all the quirky Energies
of life, ours
or a windy marsh with bitterns and ducks—that's
a business fit for a man like myself, strong & quick
as you can find, Lucy, and not to be found much longer
in the pestilent port of New York
as apprentice-clerk in a commercial house.
I did not realize how dearly I would detest it,
seventy-five thousand persons calling one place
home! & me a merchant! My life has not subdued itself
to Indigo & wine. Thoughts of thee
were like the silver thread I tied last spring
around the phoebe's leg, knotted loose
to cause no injury but to hold
forever. & soon I will return from a year
of scribbling bad english in a dim room
to show your father my worth. My sum would be
no greater for any more of that. One year given him,
Love, I offer you the rest.

Our Conspiracy of Pleasure

I came from wildness and across it, at large
among waves the size of this house, my journeys since that crossing
shorter but innumerable. I have pressed my bootsoles
into mud & moss & dry leaf duff, improvising paths
in rangy curvilinear abundance
as I followed my whim
& joy, that flew ahead, half-seen.
Your mother's frown, your father's sombre approval
blow away in the vastness where waves
lean & fall & resume, where new leaves loosen.
My hopes for us change as fast
as light on water. I am rich! You are!
Your brothers & sisters dance, the candles gutter
to their motion. Tomorrow, Lucy, Wife, we'll start
our wedding trip, sunlit, we'll wade through the shallow mist
that rises from April snow, then slide slowly
a thousand miles south,
clothes and drawings bundled,
flatboated, Ohio-floated,
Kentucky bound,
with stores of things to sell
because we must. But we will not
complicate ourselves. Let others keep the books!

III. 1808–1826

We Find the Outset Erratic

The first day the wind comes against us
so hard a man can't turn toward it & breathe,
and we tie up in the lee of a bend
since the bulky craft makes no way. Among a dozen
of us passengers only Rozier is impatient, counting the hours
as money lost. I lie with thee beneath four blankets
in the half-open cabin, pleased,
listening to twigs skitter across the canvas roof.
The wind subsides at dusk, & the river changes
its shaggy coat for close-lapped triangles
that shiver apart & reappear. Among the men
I am clairvoyant of weather, the captain's
confrère, and best
at pushing us free of mud bars.

The current is our pilot now
that moves us faster in the narrow channels
beside shrubbed islands like large animals
grazing on bottom weeds. Salt pork & biscuit
is our fare, though I volunteer to shoot a fat fresh dinner
given half an hour ashore. The captain
refuses. Let him unstick us then
at the next impasse. Are we alone
in leisureliness? Yes, & doomed I see
to an efficient honeymoon! Still
Rozier fumes. In Louisville
we'll set up shop and make him rich—he has nothing
better to do—while thou & I will study to be
Savants of happiness.

The Inn, Louisville

I feel you rend.
When I hear his cry
I think my life has flown
to another body.
And so it has.
Victor Gifford Audubon
slides into this world
on the third floor of the Indian Queen
at leaf-height, at daybreak
in my twenty-fourth year.

A Visit from Wilson

Business is a burden. We need cash.
The resolution of two unpleasantnesses
charms me with simplicity—sell the business! At last
life allows Gain and Ease to agree. Who would buy
trouble? My partner Rozier is our profit here,
who will be paid in kind for being mercenary
& Dull witted, as he showed himself again
when that odd Scotsman visited the store.
Naturalist, he called himself, & carried dozens
of drawings, Folio size. Spread on the counter
they astonished me. His best
were small-headed Flycatcher & Mississippi Kite, neither
as life-like as I have them. He talked of publication
& I was curious about his life altogether—
but Rozier, muttering the while in French
which the Scot seemed not to know,
burst out in english worse than mine
that I would have no more money to throw away
especially for silly pictures. Today the stranger
is gone, & the querulous flute from his room
late at night. Rozier sulks. The man's a mule.
I'll put this business on his back.

At Ease

If I had known such contentment existed
I would have sought it sooner. I knew
I wanted thee, & now
the home I didn't know I longed for
is real, built at Bayou Sara of logs & lichens & of our selves.
My life is with you & with my wandering,
the mill runs itself which suits me better than a store.
Geese preen in the dooryard & spread their clipped wings.
Soon Victor will be hunting bigger game
than the dozen turtles he has grabbed, giggling.
Now he watches them sun, delicious,
inconspicuous, in the fenced pond.
Johnny, who came while I was away,
is old enough just to rock & be sung to,
Sur le pont d'Avignon l'on y danse l'on y danse.
Our few disturbances are natural: storms,
& ice on the river breaking in spring
with a sound like artillery.

Disaster

I have cause to despair and will not.
I owed & was owed, availed myself of a dozen niggling Partners,
my steam Mill did worse and I was forced to sell my horses,
house, land, the unfortunate Machine itself, now stilled
except squirrel-flickered & shouted at by Jays
that eat from open sacks of grain.
Jailed for debt, I do not repent the three good years
wooden shafts turned at the center of my excursions.

The air is odd, now, empty of racket
that attended all my homecomings, grown noisier otherwise
with the children, one old enough to follow me.
He must see how few men bow to his father on the street
although I decline to notice, just as I ignored the garment
the gaoler tossed me after taking my silk shirt
to sell with all else incidental. Long hair
fell over my bare shoulders & warmed me
until Lucy brought another shirt,
less fine but my own. The sheriff said I acted like an Indian
which I will take to mean honorably & misunderstood.
I own now these clothes, one gun, drawings considered worthless
& my confidence. The drawings must be seen. I will be admired
by more than myself & family, or I mistake my efforts.

A Profitable Life

eludes me. Risen again to the world, I thought
to settle, taxidermist at the Museum in Philadelphia,
but have stuffed myself most industriously
out of business, even did fishes after all the Fowl.
The man who hired me has left and no one else
knows how to sign my name to a note? Lucy
no matter. We have been unmoneyed before.
My purpose, that had staggered,

lifts. It makes me simple, a curve
my hand draws without government by a round thought.
Enjoying my life I will enlarge it
& for this must peregrinate, reckless in others' eyes
but regular to my Plan
& you will be my astronomer, you will see its shape, my hope
realized, ah! thrush by thrush.

Portraits

I give my self a year to make one Hundred
drawings & here begin with my young friend
Joseph Mason, & Dash the game-wise dog,
our first productions a Telltale Godwit and hermit Thrush
& further a portrait of a shoemaker and his Wife
in fair trade for two pairs of boots, Dash needing none.
We take our work & comforts from the woods
as far as New Orleans, a penny between us.

We will stay the winter. I wear my good shirt
to the bookseller's to glimpse Wilson's book
which is dear. Joseph & I finish 20 drawings
including boat tailed Grackle, brown pelican
and a Warbler not described by the Scot. I am improved,
laying a ground of water colours under the pastels
to prevent appearance of the paper, but the work slows
with necessity, the city parries employment with expense.
A few warm days we set up on the street & draw from memory
faces of persons famous here, to show our skill
& have some reward. Twice we are awakened
to take likenesses of old men dying, and one clergyman
disinters his young daughter that we can preserve her Forever.
In March having made portraits everywhere
we find no more sitters & leave, pockets full of chalk.

Arrangements

The world changes in a wing beat.
Aboard a steamer, travel for me & companions
traded for three days work on a Steam Co. sign,
I meet an agreeable lady Mrs Pirrie
who much admires me as others have
and offers a position as others have not.
We talk of my project, the book I want to make
& our talk grows warmer & the air takes on
a fragrance of magnolias as we move upriver
and she, intelligent Benefactor, confirms
my belief that Fortune breathes
in each of us, if we persist: not luck
but an answer to our working joy. I am Tutor
in drawing, music & dancing, with time
to hunt & draw, & paid,
& board for Mason too. Warblers sing intermittently
among mottled beech & yellow Poplar
as we approach the settlement.